Copyright

Fruit Infused Water Recipe Book: 102+ Easy to Make, Healthy, Refreshing Vitamin Water Recipes

June 2014

Lance Devoir

Introduction

I want to thank you and congratulate you for downloading the book, The Fruit Infused Water Recipe Book.

This book contains information about fruit infused water and its benefits. This book also contains more than one hundred easy to prepare healthy fruit infused water recipes.

It is very important for us to consume enough water every day for our optimal health and body function. However, most of us do not drink enough water simply because it is tasteless. This is what makes the fruit infused water amazing. It lets you enjoy the benefits of drinking enough water per day without ever feeling that it is a chore or something that you have to do. You can consume these fruity drinks instead of drinking coffee or sodas. Drinking fruit infused water is not only fun, it also allows you to absorb the vitamins and nutrients contained in fruits. It also makes you more glowing, energetic, and healthy. Some fruit infused water has the ability to relieve stress, anxiety, and even depression.

This book contains both classic and unique fruit infused recipes that are filled with vitamins and nutrients. This book also contains tips on how to better prepare these drinks.

I hope that this book will help you jumpstart your new and healthier lifestyle.

Thanks again for downloading this book, I hope you enjoy it!

With gratitude,

Lance Devoir

Chapter 1

Why Consume Fruit Infused Water?

When we were young, we have been told that drinking water is good for us. However, because of the many other flavored and calorie-packed fluids available in the market, most of us have forgotten to drink water. We turn to sodas, coffee, and sports drinks to hydrate ourselves even when we know that these drinks can have harmful effects to our body. This is the reason why nutritionists reinvented the good old water and infused it with healthy and delicious fruits, spices, and vegetables.

Now, you can drink water and still sip something that is fruity and delicious. Here are the reasons why you should consume more fruit- infused water:

1. It can help control calories – Drinking fruit infused water will leave you feeling full most of the time. As a result, you will not consume as much food. Fruit infused water is a natural and delicious appetite suppressant.

2. It boosts metabolism – Drinking fruit infused water, especially those that are rich in Vitamin C, can help improve your

metabolism. This will later result in weight loss.

3. It maintains regularity – Drinking fruit infused water maintains regularity as it aids digestion and prevents constipation.

4. It helps remove harmful toxins from the body – Drinking fruit infused water helps flush out harmful toxins from the body. It cleanses the liver and it helps improve kidney function.

5. It relieves stress, headache, and anxiety – Some fruit infused drinks relieve stress, headache, and anxiety. These drinks will help you relax after a long day at work.

6. It helps prevent certain kinds of diseases – Fruit infused water helps strengthen the immune system. It helps fight fever, flu, cramps, and even certain heart diseases.

7. It improves skin complexion – Fruit infused water moisturizes your skin. It keeps your skin smooth, soft, and glowing. It also prevents the skin from aging and it gets rid of the ugly wrinkles.

8. It increases energy and vitality – Fruit infused drinks help ease fatigue. They also increase your energy levels and help you focus and concentrate.

9. It lightens your mood – Drinking fruit infused water helps you become more relaxed, calmer, and happier.

10. It is convenient and inexpensive – Fruit infused water is very easy to prepare. On top of that, it is also cheaper than sodas, healthy shakes, or even coffee.

Chapter 2

Refreshing and Cooling Fruit Infused Water Recipes

These fruit infused water recipes are great to consume during a hot summer day. These drinks have a cooling effect and they also have the ability to increase your energy levels and vitality.

Lemon Cucumber

This is a cooling and refreshing drink that helps you cool off and relax on a hot summer day. You can use this as a substitute and alternative to lemonade. With this drink, you get to enjoy the tangy flavor of lemonade without the added calories.

Ingredients

- 2 liters of drinking water

- 1 sliced cucumber

- 2 sliced lemons

Combine the water, cucumber and lemon in a large pitcher. Stir and cover. Refrigerate this refreshing drink for three hours. You can add ice if you like. Serve cold and enjoy!

Honeydew and Strawberry Water

This fruity drink is perfect during the hot summer. If you went out doing your grocery shopping on a hot summer day, this drink will help you relax and ease the heat.

- 1 cup of honeydew cubes

- 2 cups of sliced fresh strawberries

- 2 liters of distilled water

Add all the ingredients in a pitcher and chill in the refrigerator for about three hours. Serve and enjoy!

Lemon Raspberry Water

The combination of lemons and raspberry is quite bizarre, but the taste is just awesome. This drink is invigorating, delicious, and refreshing!

Ingredients:

- 1 lemon

- 2 cups of raspberry

- 2 liters of water

Smash the raspberries. Slice the lemons thinly. Combine the smashed raspberries, sliced lemon, and two liters of water in a pitcher and chill in the refrigerator for two to three hours. You can add ice if you like. Serve and enjoy!

Lemon Blueberry Water

This drink is loaded with Vitamin C and antioxidants. Plus, it is also very delicious and refreshing!

Ingredients:

- 2 cups of blueberries
- 1 lemon
- 2 liters of sparkling water

Thinly slice the lemon and crush the blueberries. Combine the blueberries, sparkling water, and sliced lemon in a pitcher. Add ice. Refrigerate for about two to three hours and serve.

Minty Orange Water

This drink is amazingly refreshing, and it is naturally sweet.

Ingredients:

- ½ cup of mint, chopped

- 2 liters of distilled water

- 1 orange, thinly sliced

Mix the orange, mint, and water in a pitcher. Add ice if preferred. Chill in the refrigerator for at least four hours. Serve.

Plum and Lemon Water

This drink is loaded with vitamins and minerals and it is great for the skin and the eyes. It is refreshing, too.

Ingredients:

- 2 liters of drinking water
- 4 sliced plums
- 1 thinly sliced lemon
- Ice, if preferred

Place the plums and lemon in a large pitcher. Gently muddle and mix using a spoon. Add the ice and the drinking water. Refrigerate for at least an hour before serving.

Orange Mango Tropical Water

This drink has a refreshing and fruity tropical taste. This drink is loaded with vitamins, too.

Ingredients:

- 2 liters of distilled water

- 1 orange

- 1 ripe mango

- Ice, if preferred

Cut the mango in very small pieces and thinly slice the orange. Place the sliced orange and mango in a pitcher. Add the water. Add the ice if preferred. Chill in the refrigerator for at least 2 hours. Serve and enjoy.

Melon and Rosemary Summer Water

This is a surprisingly refreshing and delicious drink. This drink is perfect for a hot and sunny day.

Ingredients:

- ½ cup of rosemary
- 1 cup of cubed watermelon
- 2 liters of distilled water

Combine the ingredients in a pitcher. Refrigerate for at least two hours before serving to your family and friends. Add ice if preferred.

Minty Strawberry Water

This is a sweet and juicy drink that people of both kids and adult can enjoy. The mint makes it more refreshing.

Ingredients:

- 2 cups of chopped strawberries

- ½ cup of chopped mint

- 2 liters of distilled water

Combine all the ingredients in a pitcher. Refrigerate this delicious minty water for at least four hours. Add ice and serve!

Refreshing Coconut Raspberry Lemon Water

This is a very healthy drink that also cleanses the body. Plus, it is amazingly refreshing and delicious.

Ingredients:

- ½ cup of coconut milk

- 1 sliced lemon

- 2 liters of distilled water

- 2 cups of raspberries

Mash the raspberries. Combine the sliced lemon, distilled water, coconut milk, and mashed raspberries in a large pitcher. Chill in the refrigerator for at least three hours. Add ice and serve.

Orange and Ginger Water

This is an amazing drink that tastes a lot like orange soda. This drink is refreshing, but this fruity sparkling drink can also ease stomachaches.

Ingredients:

- 1 inch ginger

- 2 liters of water

- 2 oranges

- Ice, if preferred

Slice the ginger and the oranges. Place all the ingredients in a pitcher and refrigerate for at least four hours before serving to your family and friends.

Minty Pineapple Water

This refreshing drink will help you beat the summer heat.

Ingredients:

- 1 cup of pineapple chunks

- 10 ripped mint leaves

- 2 liters of drinking water

- Ice, if preferred

Combine the pineapple chunks, mint leaves, ice, and drinking water in a large water pitcher. Stir gently using a spoon. Refrigerate for at least two hours before serving.

Tropical Summer Fruit Infused Water

This is a tasty and cooling drink that is perfect for the summer.

Ingredients:

- 1 cup of cubed watermelon

- 1 cup of pineapple chunks

- 2 liters of drinking water

- Ice

- 1 cup of diced mangoes

Combine the cubed watermelon, pineapple chunks, diced mangoes, and drinking water in a large water pitcher. Stir using a spoon. Chill in the refrigerator for about two hours. Serve with ice and enjoy!

Delicious and Cooling Tropical Infused Water

This is a nutritious infusion that is great for long, hot days.

Ingredients:

- 1 cup of sliced strawberries

- 1 cup of pineapple chunks

- 2 liters of drinking water

- Ice, if preferred

- 1 cup of diced mangoes

- 10 ripped mint leaves

Combine all the strawberries, pineapple chunks, drinking water, ice, mangoes, and mint leaves in a large water pitcher. Stir using a spoon. Chill in the refrigerator for about three hours before serving. Serve this drink in daintly little water bottles.

Mixed Berries and Citrus Cooling Drink

This is a refreshing, delicious, and healthy drink that can quench your thirst and beat the heat during a hot summer day. Take note that this drink is also loaded with antioxidants and can boost metabolism. This drink is perfect if you are trying to lose weight.

Ingredients:

- 1 cup of blueberries

- 1 thinly sliced lemon

- 1 cup of sliced strawberries

- 2 liters of drinking water

- 1 cup of raspberries

- 1 thinly sliced lemon

- 1 thinly sliced tangerine

Combine all the ingredients in a large water pitcher. Stir using a wooden spoon. Chill in the refrigerator for about three hours before serving. Serve in dainty little water bottles to make the drink look more appetizing and stylish.

Pineapple, Orange, and Mango Infused Water

This is a classic refreshing drink that is delicious and loaded with vitamins and nutrients.

Ingredients:

- 1 cup of pineapple chunks

- 1 thinly sliced orange

- 1 cup of diced mangoes

- 2 liters of drinking water

- Ice

Combine the pineapple chunks, orange, water, ice, and mangoes in a large water pitcher. Chill in the refrigerator for at least one hour before serving to your family and guests.

Chapter 3

Metabolism-Boosting Fruit Infused Water Recipes

These fruit-infused water recipes can boost your metabolism and aid weight loss. You can place these refreshing drinks in stylish water bottles and consume when exercising or working.

Lime and Apple Infused Water

This drink is refreshing and delicious. But more than that, it is loaded with Vitamin C. This drink helps improve the body's metabolism and it helps lower down the cholesterol level. This drink is perfect If you are trying to lose weight.

Ingredients:

- 2 liters of distilled water

- 1 sliced lime

- 2 sliced apples

- Ice

Place the lime and apples in a large pitcher and mix using a spoon. Add the water and ice and refrigerate for about 1 to 2 hours before serving. You can keep this drink for about two days and you can keep refilling it.

Cucumber and Chili Water

This is a great drink that is perfect if you are trying to lose weight. This drink boosts metabolism. This amazing drink also strengthens the immune system and it improves your vitality and energy level.

Ingredients:

- 2 liters of drinking water

- 4 thinly chopped chilies

- 1 thinly sliced cucumber

- Ice, if preferred

Combine the cucumber and chilies in a large pitcher. Add the ice and the drinking water. Chill in the refrigerator for at least thirty minutes. Serve and enjoy!

Lemon and Ginger Water

This drink is energizing and it has many health benefits. This drink can serve as a pain reliever to those who are suffering from stomachache. This drink also helps improve the body's metabolism. Thus, this drink is perfect if you are trying to lose weight.

Ingredients:

- 3 inch ginger, thinly sliced and peeled

- 1 thinly sliced lemon

- 2 liters of distilled water

- Ice, if preferred

Combine the ginger and lemon in a large pitcher. Mix using a spoon. Add the water and ice. Chill in the refrigerator for about two hours before serving to your family and friends. It is best to consume this drink in the morning.

Coco Blueberry Water

Coconut water is one of the healthiest plant juices on Earth. This coconut and blueberry combination is not only delicious, it also helps improve your body's metabolism and it is perfect if you are trying to lose weight.

Ingredients:

- 2 pints of coconut water

- 1 cup of blueberries

Place the blueberries in a large pitcher and gently mash it using a wooden spoon or spatula. Add the coconut water and mix well. Chill this mixture in the refrigerator before serving

Minty Lemon, Cucumber, and Lime Water

This drink boosts the body's metabolism. But, it has also many other benefits. This energizing and refreshing drink is great for your immune system and skin.

Ingredients:

- 1 thinly sliced cucumber

- 10 crushed mint leaves

- 1 sliced lemon

- 2 liters of distilled water

- 2 sliced limes

Combine all the ingredients in a pitcher. Refrigerate for about 2 hours before serving. Add ice if preferred.

Pomegranate Lemon Water

This amazing drink boosts metabolism and helps the body burn fats. It is also great for the skin and if you consume it regularly, you will feel and look younger.

Ingredients:

- 2 liters of distilled water

- 1 cup of pomegranate seeds

- ¼ thinly sliced lemon

- Ice, if preferred

Combine the pomegranate seeds and sliced lemon in a large pitcher. Mix gently. Add the water and ice. Chill in the refrigerator for at least one hour before serving. You can consume this drink in the morning or after exercising.

Ginger and Pear Water

Pears are great for weight loss. It also helps reduce the bad cholesterol level in the body. This refreshing drink has a certain kick and this is perfect if you want to improve your body's metabolism.

Ingredients:

- 2 liters of water

- 10 sliced pears

- ½ cup of sliced and peeled ginger

Mix all the ingredients and chill for about six hours. Serve.

Peach, Vanilla, and Basil Water

This healthy drink is great for weight loss. When consumed regularly, this drink can also have great effects to your skin. Moreover, this drink helps relieve stress and other stress related diseases.

Ingredients:

- 2 liters of distilled water

- 2 sliced peaches

- 1 halved vanilla bean

- 10 torn basil leaves

- Ice, if preferred

Combine the basil leaves, peaches, and vanilla bean in a large pitcher. Mix using a spatula or wooden spoon. Add the distilled water and ice. Chill in the refrigerator for about two hours. Serve and enjoy!

Lemon, Ginger, and Blackberry Water

This drink detoxifies the body and it is a great supplement for weight loss. This drink is also perfect for women who frequently suffer from PMS or Premenstrual Syndrome.

Ingredients:

- 1 sliced lemon

- 2 liters of water

- 3 inch sliced ginger

- 2 cups of blackberries

- Ice, if preferred

Combine the lemon, blackberries, and ginger in a pitcher. Mix using a spatula or wooden spoon. Add the ice and water. Chill in the refrigerator for about one hour before serving.

Tangerine, Thyme, and Fennel Water

This drink is filled with Vitamin C and it aids metabolism. This drink is not only refreshing and thirst-quenching, it also helps people lose weight.

Ingredients:

- 2 liters of distilled water

- 1 shaved fennel bulb

- 4 thyme sprigs

- 6 zested tangerines

Combine the fennel, thyme, tangerines, and water in a pitcher. Chill in a refrigeration for about six hours. For best results, strain using a mesh before serving.

Lemon Grass and Cucumber

This is an amazing detoxifying drink that can relieve anxiety and stress. This drink is incredibly soothing and relaxing. It also improves memory and relieves certain body pains. More importantly, this drink is great for people who want to lose weight.

Ingredients:

- 1 sliced cucumber

- 2 liters of distilled water

- Ice, if preferred

- 2 stalks of lemongrass

Smash the lemon grass using a rolling pin. Combine the cucumber, lemon grass, water, and ice in a large pitcher. Chill in the refrigerator for at least one hour before serving.

Grape and Cucumber Infused Water

This drink can help you lose weight. In addition to that, it strengthens the immune system and makes your bones and joints healthier.

Ingredients:

- 2 liters of distilled water

- 1 cup of halved grapes

- 1 thinly sliced cucumber

- Ice, if preferred

Mix the halved grapes and cucumber in a large water pitcher using a spatula or wooden spoon. Add the water and ice. Place in the refrigerator for about two hours before serving.

You can actually keep this drink for about two to three days in the refrigerator and you can refill it many times.

Lavender, Cucumber, and Mint Water

This drink has many health benefits. It can ease PMS or Premenstrual Syndrome, bad breath, and some major digestive problems. This fruit infused water is also good for the skin. If you drink this regularly, your skin will be more glowing and healthy. This drink can also be used for weight loss. Most of all, it has a refreshing and minty taste.

Ingredients:

- 2 liters of distilled water

- 1 sprig of lavender

- 1 thinly sliced cucumber

- 2 sprigs of mint

- Ice, if preferred

Combine the lavender, cucumber, and mint in a large pitcher using a spatula or wooden spoon. Do this until you can smell the aroma. Add the ice and the water and refrigerate for about an hour before serving.

Minty Honeydew Water

This drink boosts your metabolism and it has a very sweet, sugary, and minty taste. It is also a cocktail of different kinds of melon fruits!

Ingredients:

- 1 pound of cubed seedless watermelon

- One half cup of mint leaves

- One half cubed honeydew melon

- 2 liters of distilled water

- 1 cubed cantaloupe

- Ice, if preferred

Combine the watermelon, cantaloupe, water, honeydew melon, and ice in a large pitcher. Stir and chill in the refrigerator for about one hour before serving. You can garnish this drink with other fruits, if you like.

Kiwi and Lavender Infused Water

This drink is not only delicious and sweet, it is also very good to look at. The flavors of lavender and blend perfectly.

Ingredients:

- 2 tablespoons of crushed lavender leaves

- 4 ripe kiwis

- Ice, if preferred

- Two liters of distilled water

Clean the kiwis and cut into chunky slices. Place the lavender and kiwis in a pitcher and mix lightly using a spatula or wooden spoon. Add water and ice and refrigerate for about three hours. Strain the water using a mesh and serve.

Strawberry and Melon Infused Water

This drink is a great metabolism booster and it is refreshing, cooling, and delicious, too. This drink can also give you lots of energy so it is best to carry this around in a water container when exercising. This will ensure that you will get the most from the exercise plus this will give you more energy that you will need to complete your workout routine for the day.

Ingredients:

- One half honeydew melon

- One half watermelon

- Two liters of distilled water

- One cup of strawberries

- Ice, if preferred

Slice the strawberries and melons in cubes. Combine all the ingredients in a large pitcher. It is best to refrigerate this drink in the refrigerator for about thirty minutes before serving.

Cucumber and Peach Water

If you do not like fruit infused drinks that are sweet, this is the perfect for you. The cucumber makes the drink really cool and refreshing. This drink also improves your body's metabolism.

Ingredients:

- 1 sliced cucumber

- 2 sliced peaches

- 2 liters of distilled water

- Ice, if preferred

Combine all the ingredients in a large pitcher. Cover the pitcher and chill in the refrigerator for at least an hour before serving. You may garnish this drink with other fruits, flowers, or herbs.

Apple and Blueberry Infused Water

This combination of apple and blueberry is a bit bizarre, but it tastes good. This drink is good for your skin, but more than that, it can also improve your metabolism.

Ingredients:

- 2 cups of slightly mashed blueberries

- 1 cubed apple

- 2 liters of distilled water

- Ice, if preferred

Combine the ingredients in a large pitcher. Stir using a wooden spoon or spatula. Chill in the refrigerator for three to four hours before serving.

Hawaii- Style Pineapple and Blueberry Infused Water

It is best to consume this refreshing and delicious drink early in the morning. This drink is rich in vitamin C and it improves the metabolism.

Ingredients:

- 1 cup of ice

- 2 liter of distilled water

- 1 cup of pineapple chunks

- 1 cup of blueberries

Combine all the ingredients in a pitcher. Remember to serve this drink cold so the water would absorb the flavors better. Chill in the refrigerator for at least thirty minutes for best results.

Clementine, Pear, and Cranberry Infused Water

This drink is full of amazing, natural flavors. This drink is delicious, refreshing, and it helps enhance your body's metabolism.

Ingredients:

- 3 tablespoons of dried cranberries

- 2 sliced pears

- 2 cuts of Clementine

- 2 liters of distilled water

- Ice, if preferred

- 2 teaspoons of allspice berries

It is best to thinly slice the fruits to release the flavors. You can also add other fruits like apple or mango if you like. Combine all the ingredients in a pitcher. Chill in the refrigerator for about three hours before serving.

Sage and Grapefruit Metabolism Boosting Water

Many studies show that Grapefruit is great for weight loss because it reduce the insulin levels in the body. Sage is also good for weight loss, so this combination is best if you really need help in jump starting your weight loss plan. You can consume this drink to keep yourself hydrated during a long workout session.

Ingredients:

- 4 teaspoons of sage

- 2 cups of grapefruit

- 2 liters of distilled water

Place the grapefruit in a pitcher. Mash it using a spatula or wooden spoon to release the flavor. Crush the sage and add it to the grapefruit. Add the water and chill for about one hour before serving. You can add ice, if preferred.

Ginger and Mango Water

This is a popular recipe that can boost your metabolism. This drink can also be a great pain reliever for menstrual cramps, morning sickness, and migraines.

Ingredients:

- 1 cup of cubed mangoes

- 3 inch sliced ginger

- 2 liters of distilled water

Combine all the ingredients in a pitcher. Chill for around an hour before serving.

Cinnamon and Apple Infused Water

This is also a popular recipe that is great for weight loss. This drink is also sweet and full of flavor.

Ingredients:

- 1 cinnamon stick

- 2 liters of distilled water

- Ice, if preferred

- 1 apple

Thinly slice the apple and place it in a large water pitcher. Add the cinnamon stick, ice, and water. Refrigerate this drink for about one hour before serving. You can place this in a water bottle and consume this while working or exercising.

Amazing Grapefruit, Pineapple, and Apple Infused Water

Grapefruit and apple can boost your body's metabolism and these fruits have the ability to curb your appetite. By drinking this fruit infused water, you will consume less food.

Ingredients:

- 1 grapefruit

- 1 green apple

- 1 fresh pineapple

- 2 liters of distilled water

- Ice

Slice the grapefruit, pineapple, and apple. Place the ingredients in an attractive water pitcher. Squeeze the pineapple slices lightly if you want to boost the flavor. Chill in the refrigerator for about 4 hours before serving.

Tangerine and Strawberry Infused Water

This is a refreshing drink that is rich in Vitamin C. This drink boosts metabolism and promotes weight loss. If you want to lose weight fast, drink one liter of this fruit infused water daily.

Ingredients:

- 1 sliced tangerine

- 1 cup of sliced dried strawberries

- 2 liters of distilled water

Combine all ingredients in a pitcher. You can serve this hot or cold. If you prefer to serve this drink cold, refrigerate for at least one hour before serving.

Mojito and Honeydew Metabolism Boosting Water

This drink can be used as a "workout" water. This drink boosts metabolism.

Ingredients:

- 2 liters of distilled water

- 8 mint leaves

- 1 cup of sliced honeydew lemon

- 1 thinly sliced lime

- Ice, if preferred

Combine all the ingredients in a large water pitcher. Mix and chill in the refrigerator for at least 30 minutes before serving.

Chapter 4

Skin-Glowing Fruit Infused Water Recipes

These delicious water infused water recipes have many skin benefits. These refreshing drinks can moisturize the skin and make it look younger and healthier. These drinks are also filled with vitamins that help fight free radicals and repair damaged cells.

Kiwi and Strawberry Invigorating Infused Water

This is a classic drink that is loaded with vitamin E and vitamin A. This drink cleanses the colon, fights free radicals, and it is really great for the skin.

Ingredients:

- 4 strawberries

- 2 liters of distilled water

- 4 kiwis

- Ice, preferred

Slice the strawberries and kiwis into cubes. Place the fruits in a large pitcher. Mix and add the water. Add ice, if preferred. Chill in the refrigerator for at least four hours before serving. This will ensure that the flavors and nutrients have been absorbed by the water.

Lime, blackberry, and Cherry Infused Water

This is an incredibly delicious drink. Plus, this is really good for the skin.

Ingredients:

- 1 cup of blackberries

- 2 limes

- 1 cup of cherries

- 2 liters of distilled water

- Ice, if preferred

Thinly slice the limes. Place it in a large pitcher. Add the cherries, water, ice, and blackberries. Chill in the refrigerator for at least one hour before serving.

Orange and Cranberry Skin Invigorating Water

This drink is good for the skin and it also helps relieve anxiety and stress.

Ingredients:

- 1 cup of cranberries

- 2 liters of distilled water

- 2 sliced oranges

- Ice, if preferred

Combine all the ingredients in a large water pitcher. Chill in the refrigerator for about 2 hours before serving.

Basil, Lemon, Ginger, and Cucumber Water

This drink is invigorating and it is great for the skin. This drink is also best for people who are not fond of fruity and sweet drinks.

Ingredients:

- 1 thinly sliced cucumber

- 2 inches of sliced and peeled ginger

- 1 thinly sliced lemon

- 8 basil leaves

- 2 liters of distilled water

Combine all the ingredients in a water pitcher. Mix using a spatula or a wooden spoon. Refrigerate this drink for about 2 hours before serving.

Minty Blackberry Infused Water

This drink can be used for weight loss. But, this is also great for the skin. It fights free radicals causing your skin to look fresh and younger.

Ingredients:

- 5 torn mint leaves

- 2 liters of distilled water

- ½ cup of blackberries

- Ice if preferred

Place the mint leaves and blackberries in a large water pitcher. Gently mix using a spatula or wooden spoon until you could smell the relaxing scent of mint. Add the water and ice. Chill this drink in the refrigerator for at least an hour before serving.

Minty Cucumber and Watermelon Water

If you want to have a healthy looking skin, this drink is for you.

Ingredients:

- 1 cup of watermelon

- 2 liters of drinking water

- 1 thinly sliced cucumber

- Ice, if preferred

- 10 torn mint leaves

Place the cucumber, watermelon, and mint in a large pitcher. Gently mix the three ingredients until you can smell the aroma of mint. Add the ice and drinking water. Chill this drink for at least an hour before serving.

Lemon and Basil Invigorating Water

This drink is energizing and invigorating. It also keeps your skin looking young. This drink can also help you lose weight. This drink can also help you relax and relieve stress.

Ingredients:

- 1 sliced lemon

- 2 liters of distilled water

- 20 torn basil leaves

- Ice, if preferred

Combine the water, ice, lemon, and basil leaves in a pitcher. Gently mix and stir using a wooden spoon. Chill in the refrigerator for about thirty minutes before serving.

Anti- Aging Lime and Ginger Water

This drink is great for your skin and it has anti-aging benefits.

Ingredients:

- 3 inches sliced and peeled ginger

- 1 thinly sliced lime

- 2 liters of distilled water

- Ice, if preferred

Combine all the ingredients in a large water pitcher. Chill in the refrigerator for at least two hours before serving. Serve in beautiful glass water bottles.

Healthy Cilantro, Orange, Lemon, and Lime Infused Water

This citrus drink is loaded with Vitamin C. This is great for the skin and it is also good for people who have a urinary tract infection or UTI and kidney stones. This drink can also reduce inflammation and it is extremely relaxing.

Ingredients:

- 1 thinly sliced orange

- 1 thinly sliced lime

- 2 liters of distilled water

- 1 thinly sliced lemon

- Ice, if preferred

- One fourth cup of crushed cilantro leaves

Combine the orange, lime, lemon, and cilantro leaves in a large water pitcher. Mix using a wooden spoon or a spatula. Add the distilled water and ice. Chill in the refrigerator for at least one hour before serving.

Minty Cranberry and Lemon Infused Water

This minty drink is good for weight loss. But, this drink is loaded with vitamins that makes your skin glow and look better. If you drink this daily, you will notice its skin benefits in just a few days.

Ingredients:

- 1 cup of cranberries

- 2 liters of distilled water

- ½ thinly sliced lemon

- Ice, if preferred

- 10 torn mint leaves

Combine all the ingredients in a water pitcher. Stir and mix using a wooden spoon or spatula. Chill in the refrigerator for at least two hours before serving. This will ensure that the flavors and nutrients have been absorbed by the water.

Energizing and Invigorating Lime and Cucumber Water

This drink is energizing and it can also do wonders for your skin. Many people also use this drink to cure hangovers and migraines.

Ingredients:

- 1 thinly sliced cucumber

- 2 liters of distilled water

- 1 thinly sliced lime

- Ice, if preferred

Combine all the ingredients in a large water pitcher. Stir using a spatula. Chill in the refrigerator for at least one hour before serving. Serve in beautiful glass water bottles.

Mint and Cantaloupe Infused Water

Aside from the fact that this drink can make your skin glow with health, this invigorating drink has a lot of other health benefits. This is great for people who suffer from asthma and other lung diseases. It also aids digestion. This drink is also relaxing and perfect after a long stressful workday.

Ingredients:

- 6 torn mint leaves

- 2 liters of distilled water

- 1 cup of cubed cantaloupe

- Ice, if preferred

Place the mint leaves and cantaloupe in a large water pitcher. Mix using spatula or wooden spoon until you can smell the relaxing aroma of mint. Chill in the refrigerator for at least one hour before serving. Serve this drink in beautiful glass water glasses.

Cucumber and Lavender Water

This drink makes the skin look healthy and glowing. This infused water is also good for people who have digestive problems.

Ingredients:

- 2 sprigs of lavender

- 2 liters of distilled water

- 1 thinly sliced cucumber

- Ice, if preferred

Combine the lavender, cucumber, water, and ice in a large pitcher. Stir using a wooden spoon or spatula. Chill this drink for at least one hour before serving. The lavenders will look great when served in small glass water bottles.

Tangerine, Lime, and Ginger Infused Water

This drink is filled with vitamins that will help your skin look better and younger. This drink is also known to help cure cold and flu. Aside from its skin benefits, this could also help you lose weight.

Ingredients:

- 1 thinly sliced lime

- 2 liters of distilled water

- 1 thinly sliced tangerine

- 3 inch ginger

- Ice, if preferred

Combine the lime, tangerine, ginger, water, and ice in a large water pitcher. Chill in the refrigerator for at least two hours. Serve and enjoy!

Orange and Mango Water

This infused water is rich in Vitamin C. It is great for the skin and it strengthens your immune system.

Ingredients:

- 4 thinly sliced kiwis

- 2 liters of distilled water

- 2 mangoes, sliced into cubes

- Ice, if preferred

Combine all the ingredients in a large pitcher. Stir using a spatula and wooden spoon. Chill in the refrigerator for at least two hours.

Cucumber, Cantaloupe, Honeydew, and Watermelon Water

This fruity drink is great for the skin. It also tastes good and it relieves headaches, migraines, and extreme hangover.

Ingredients:

- 1 cup of cubed cantaloupe

- 1 cup of cubed honeydew

- 2 liters of distilled water

- 1 cup of cubed watermelon

- 1 thinly sliced cucumber

- Ice, if preferred

Combine the cantaloupe, honeydew, watermelon, cucumber, ice, and water in a large pitcher. Stir using a spatula. Chill in the refrigerator for at least two hours before serving.

Lemon, Lemongrass, and Cucumber Water

This amazing, invigorating drink is good for the skin. The lemongrass also helps relieves anxiety, stress, and worry. Drinking this infused water is one of the best ways to cap a long, stressful day.

Ingredients:

- 1 thinly sliced lemon

- 1 thinly sliced cucumber

- 2 stalks of lemongrass

- 2 liters of distilled water

- Ice, if preferred

Cut the lemon grass in half and smash it using a rolling pin. Place the lemongrass in a large water pitcher. Add the cucumber, lemon, water, and ice. Stir using a spatula. Chill in the refrigerator for at least one hour before serving. Serve in pretty glass water bottles.

Tropical Pineapple and Mango Water

This drink has a calming and it is great for the skin. This drink also has a sweet tropical taste and would go well with any meal.

Ingredients:

- 1 cup of cubed pineapple

- 1 cup of cubed mango

- Ice, if preferred

- 2 liters of distilled water

Combine the pineapple, ice, mango, and water in a large pitcher. Stir using a spatula or any wooden spoon. Refrigerate for about an hour before serving.

Cucumber, Rosemary, and Lemon Infused Water

This drink strengthens the immune system. It is also great for the skin. This drink is also refreshing and this will give you a healthy glow when consumed regularly.

Ingredients:

- 1 thinly sliced cucumber

- 1 thinly sliced lemon

- 2 liters of distilled water

- 2 crushed sprigs of rosemary

- Ice, if preferred

Combine the cucumber, rosemary, and lemon in a large water pitcher. Mix using a spatula or wooden spoon. Add the water and ice. Stir and cover. Chill this drink for at least two hours before serving. This will ensure that the flavors and nutrients are absorbed by the water. Serve in beautiful glass water bottles.

Skin Invigorating Papaya, Lime, and Ginger Infused Water

This drink invigorates the skin and it has many other health benefits, too. This drink also strengthens the immune system and digestive system.

Ingredients:

- 1 cup of cubed papaya

- 2 inches of peeled and sliced ginger root

- 1 thinly sliced lime

- 2 liters of distilled water

- Ice, if preferred

Combine the sliced ginger, lime, papaya, ice, and water in a large pitcher. Chill in the refrigerator for at about two hours before serving. Serve in beautiful water glasses and enjoy!

Orange, Lime, and Plum Water

This is a very delicious drink that is good for your skin. Since this drink is also filled with Vitamin C, this drink also aids weight loss and can boost your metabolism.

Ingredients:

- 1 thinly sliced lime

- 2 liters of distilled water

- 4 thinly sliced plums

- 1 thinly sliced orange

- Ice, if preferred

Combine the lime, water, ice, plums, oranges, and water in a large pitcher. Chill in a refrigerator for at least one hour before serving. This drink really looks good and refreshing when served in dainty glass water bottles.

Mint and Lavender Water

This minty drink can be very beneficial to your skin. This drink can also relieve depression, anxiety, and memory problems.

Ingredients:

- 2 sprigs of mint

- 2 liters of water

- Ice, if preferred

- 1 sprig of lavender

Place the mint and the lavender in a large water pitcher. Gently mix using a wooden spoon or spatula to release the flavors and aroma. Add ice and water. Stir and refrigerate for about one hour. Serve and enjoy!

Lime, Raspberry, and Blueberry Infused Water

This is a very delicious fruity drink that is filled with antioxidants. This is great for the skin as it prevents skin aging. If consumed regularly, you will notice a different kind of glow in your skin.

Ingredients:

- ½ cup of blueberries

- 1 thinly sliced lime

- ½ cup of raspberry

- 1 liter of distilled water

- Ice, if preferred

Combine the raspberry, blueberries, water, lime, and ice in a water pitcher. Gently stir using a spatula or wooden spoon. Chill this drink in the refrigerator for about two hours before consuming. This drink will also look good and appetizing when served in beautiful water glasses.

Lime, Cranberry, Blueberry, and Orange Water

This is another fruity drink that is great for your skin. This drink tastes good and it has also anti-aging benefits. It is filled with vitamin C and antioxidants. Aside from its skin benefits, this drink can also relieve stress. You can consume this drink after a long day at work.

Ingredients:

- 1 cup of cranberries

- 2 liters of distilled water

- 1 thinly sliced lime

- 1 cup of blueberries

- 1 thinly sliced orange

- Ice, if preferred

Combine the lime, cranberries, orange, water, ice, and blueberries in a large water pitcher. Gently stir using a spatula or wooden spoon. Chill this fruity drink in the refrigerator for about two hours before serving. Serve this in dainty little glass water bottles.

Chapter 5

Detoxifying Fruit Infused Water Recipes

These delicious and tasty fruit infused water recipes have the ability to flush out harmful toxins from your body. These healthy drinks can cleanse your colon and your kidneys. These drinks are filled with antioxidants. Drinking detoxifying fruit infused water daily will ensure that you are always in good shape.

Grapefruit and Grape Detoxifying Water

This drink is great for cleansing your body and removing the toxic elements in our body. It also strengthens the immune system and improves kidney health. This drink also has anti-aging benefits.

Ingredients:

- 1 cup of halved seedless grapes

- 2 liters of distilled water

- ½ sliced grapefruit

- Ice if preferred

Making this detoxifying drink is really easy. Just combine all the ingredients in a water pitcher and then, chill in a refrigerator for about two hours before serving.

Detoxifying Kiwi and Watermelon Infused Water

This delicious detoxifying drink is rich in vitamins that strengthen the immune system. This drink also improves your heart health.

Ingredients:

- 2 liters of distilled water

- 4 thinly sliced kiwis

- Ice, if preferred

- 1 cup of cubed watermelon (Make sure to remove the seeds)

Combine the kiwis, water, watermelon, and ice is a large water pitcher. Gently stir using a spatula or wooden spoon. Chill in the refrigerator for at least two hours before serving.

Kiwi Cucumber Detox Water

This drink is tasty, delicious, and it cleanses the body. It is best to consume this drink in the morning right after waking up. This drink is also invigorating and drinking this detox water is a great way to start your day.

Ingredients:

- 2 liters of drinking water

- 4 thinly sliced kiwis

- ½ thinly sliced cucumber

- 2 diced sprigs of mint

- Ice, if preferred

Combine the water, ice, kiwis, cucumber, and mint in a large water pitcher. Stir with spatula or wooden spoon. Chill in the refrigerator overnight before consuming in the morning.

Watermelon and Mint Detox Water

This is one of the more popular detoxifying fruit-infused water today. This is easy to make and it repairs damaged body cells. This detoxifying drink also improves liver function.

Ingredients:

- 1 cup of cubed watermelon

- 6 mint leaves

- 2 liters of drinking water

- Ice, if preferred

Combine the water, ice, mint leaves, and watermelon in a large pitcher. Gently stir the ingredients with a spatula or wooden spoon. Chill in the refrigerator overnight before consuming. It is important to strain the water before serving.

Pineapple, Lemon, and Pomegranate Detoxifying Water

This detox drink has amazing cleansing power. This drink also reduces the risk of heart diseases and can prevent certain kinds of cancer.

Ingredients:

- 2 liters of distilled water

- 4 cups of chopped pineapple

- 4 inches of sliced ginger

- 2 cups of sliced pomegranate

- 2 thinly sliced lemon

- Ice, if preferred

Combine the ginger, pineapple, pomegranate, lemon, water, and ice in a large water pitcher. Gently mix and stir using a spatula or wooden spoon. Refrigerate for about three hours before serving. Serve in beautiful glass water bottles.

Detoxifying Citrus Water

This delicious and refreshing citrus drink is rejuvenating and relaxing. It cleanses and detoxifies the body, too.

Ingredients:

- 1 smashed grapefruit

- One half sliced banana

- 1 smashed orange

- 2 liters of distilled water

- Ice, if preferred

Combine the banana, orange, grapefruit, water, and ice in a large pitcher. Mix and stir using a spatula or wooden spoon. Chill in the refrigerator for about two hours before serving.

Minty Coco Citrus Water

This is an amazing drink minty drink that helps fight the free radicals in your body. This drink cleanses your body and it is also refreshing. You can drink this in the morning or you can consume this after a long workday.

Ingredients:

- 1 thinly sliced orange

- 10 mint leaves

- 2 liters of distilled water

- 1 cup of coconut water

- Ice, if preferred

Combine the sliced orange, mint leaves, distilled water, coconut water, and ice in a large water pitcher. Mix the ingredient using spatula or a wooden spoon. Chill in the refrigerator for about three hours before serving. You can serve this in dainty glass water bottles.

Cherry and Banana Detox Drink

This is a sweet fruit infused water that is not only delicious; it also detoxifies and cleanses the body.

Ingredients:

- 2 liters of distilled water

- 2 slightly mashed bananas

- 2 cups of slightly mashed cherries

- Ice, if preferred

Combine the bananas, cherries, water, and ice in a large pitcher. Stir using a spatula or wooden spoon. Cover and chill for at least five hours before serving.

Pineapple and Ginger Water

This is a refreshing detox drink that you can enjoy after waking up in the morning. This drink is both sweet and spicy and it has the ability to cleanse your body.

Ingredients:

- ½ cup of cubed pineapples

- ½ inch of sliced and peeled ginger

- 1 liter of distilled water

- Ice, if preferred

Combine the cubed pineapples, ginger, water, and ice in a water pitcher. Gently stir using a spatula or wooden spoon. Chill this detoxifying drink in the refrigerator for about three hours before consuming.

Berry Cocktail Detox Water

This is a very delicious drink that combines four types of berries. This drink is rich in vitamins and antioxidants. It cleanses the body and make the skin look younger. This drink looks great, too. You can serve this during parties and get-togethers.

Ingredients:

- One half cup of strawberries

- One half cup of blueberries

- One half cup of blackberries

- One half cup of cranberries

- 2 liters of distilled water

- Ice, if preferred

Slice each berry into four pieces. Combine the strawberries, blackberries, blueberries, water, ice, and cranberries in a large water pitcher. Gently stir using a spoon or a spatula. Chill in the refrigerator overnight before consuming in the morning.

Beet, Strawberry, Banana, and Pineapple Detox Drinks

This drink is rich in nutrients and it is really delicious. This fruity drink is rich in antioxidants and it has the ability to cleanse the body.

Ingredients:

- 1 banana

- 3 liters of water

- One half cup of pineapple

- ½ cup of strawberries

Peel the beets and remove the stem and leaves. Slice the pineapple, strawberries, and banana. Combine all the ingredients in a large pitcher. Chill in the refrigerator for at least three hours before serving.

Banana and Citrus Detox Drink

This recipe is very popular because it is really delicious. It is very refreshing and this is perfect to consume during the summer. This drink cleanses and removes the harmful toxins in the body. This drink is also rich in Vitamin C which means that this drink can also help you lose weight.

Ingredients:

- 4 sliced bananas

- 2 thinly sliced oranges

- 1 thinly sliced lemon

- 2 liters of water

- Ice, if preferred

- 2 thinly sliced tangerines

- 1 thinly sliced lime

Combine the bananas, lime, lemon, oranges, tangerines, water, and ice in a large water pitcher. Gently stir the mixture using a spatula or a wooden spoon. Chill and store in the refrigerator overnight before consuming. Serve in small and beautiful glass water bottles.

Apple, Lemon, Beets, and Ginger Liver Detox Water

This drink cleanses the liver and detoxify the body. It also increases the body's metabolism. If you have been consuming alcohol and unhealthy foods over the years, it is time to take care of your liver by consuming this healthy detox drink regularly.

Ingredients:

- 1 lemon

- 2 beets

- 1 red apple

- 1 green apple

- 1 inch of ginger root

- 2 liters of distilled water

Grate the ginger. Slice the lemon thinly and slice the apples into chunks. Combine the water, ice, ginger, lemon, and apples in a large water pitcher. Refrigerate for about three hours. Strain the water. Serve and enjoy!

Detoxifying Blueberry and Cranberry Water

This is a great fusion of flavors. This drink removes the harmful toxins in the body and fight free radicals. This delicious drink is filled with vitamins and nutrients increases your energy and vitality.

Ingredients:

- 2 thinly sliced bananas

- 1 cup of blueberries

- 2 liters of sparkling water

- ½ cup of cranberries

- 1 cup of coconut water

- Ice, preferred

Combine the blueberries, bananas, sparkling water, ice, coconut water, and cranberries. Stir the mixture gently using a spatula or a spoon. Store this drink in the refrigerator overnight before consuming.

Strawberry, Grapefruit, and Avocado Morning Detox Drink

This drink is sweet and really tasty. This drink is loaded with vitamins and nutrients. It is also great for the skin and can help you lose weight. Think drink can also cure a terrible hangover.

Ingredients:

- 2 cups of sliced grapefruit

- 1 sliced avocado

- 1 cup of sliced strawberry

- 1 cup of orange chunks

- 1 cup of banana

- 2 liters of distilled water

- Ice, if preferred

Combine the avocado, strawberry, banana, grapefruit, orange, ice, and water in a large water pitcher. Chill in the refrigerator for about three hours. Serve in beautiful little bottles and enjoy!

Minty and Fruity Detox Drink

This drink is hydrating and this could be used as an exercise water. This delicious drink can cleanse the body and flush out the harmful toxins in the body. It is also a relaxing and refreshing drink that you can consume in the middle of a hot summer day.

Ingredients:

- 2 sliced apples

- ½ cup of strawberries

- 4 mint leaves

- 3 thinly sliced cucumbers

- Ice, if preferred

- 2 liters of drinking water

Combine the strawberries, apples, mint, cucumbers, ice, and water in a large water pitcher. Gently stir using a spatula or spoon. Chill in the refrigerator in about three hours before consuming.

Hydrating and Detoxifying Fruit Cocktail

This drink cleanses and detoxifies the body. It is also refreshing and delicious. You can consume this healthy drink all day long.

Ingredients:

- 2 sliced apples

- 2 sliced cucumbers

- ½ cup of strawberries

- ½ cup of cubed seedless watermelon

- 2 liters of drinking water

- Ice, if preferred

Combine the apples, strawberries, cucumbers, watermelon, water and ice in a large water pitcher. Gently stir the mixture using a wooden spoon or a spatula. Chill in the refrigerator for about three hours before serving.

Lemon and Strawberry Detox Tea

This hot drink is tasty and delicious. It also helps cleanse the body and remove the harmful toxins. This detox drink is also rich in Vitamin C.

Ingredients:

- Lemonade Tea mixture

- 2 liters of drinking water

- 2 sliced lemons

- One cup of sliced strawberries

Boil the water and place the tea in the boiling water. Set this aside for a few minutes. Pour the tea into a large water pitcher. Add the strawberries and lemons. Chill this tea mixture in the refrigerator for about three hours before serving.

Fruit and Vegetable Detoxifying Drink

This fruit and vegetable infused water is sweet and it helps flush out those harmful toxins that our body has accumulated. This drink also looks attractive and appetizing and it is best to consume this drink in small and dainty glass water bottles.

Ingredients:

- 4 apples, sliced into 4 pieces each

- 2 liters of drinking water

- 8 thinly sliced limes

- 4 sliced carrots

- 2 sliced celery stalks

- Ice, if preferred

Combine the apples, limes, carrots, ice, celery, and water in a large water pitcher. Gently stir using a spatula or a spoon. Chill in the refrigerator for about 4 hours before serving. Serve and enjoy!

Strawberry and Grape Detox Water

This is a very healthy, detoxifying drink that is rich in vitamins and certain antioxidants. This drink helps fight free radicals in your body and it is refreshing, too.

Ingredients:

- 1 cup of grapes (Each grape should be sliced into half)

- 1 cup of strawberries (Each Strawberry should be sliced into half)

- 2 liters of drinking water

- Ice, if preferred

- 4 ripped mint leaves

Combine the grapes, drinking water, mint, ice, and strawberries in a large pitcher. Stir using a wooden spoon or a spatula. Chill this drink in the refrigerator for at least three hours before serving.

Chapter 6

Stress Relieving Fruit Infused Water Recipes

If you have a stressful job or you are going through a stressful and difficult time in your life, you should try these stress relieving fruit infused water recipes. These fruit infused drinks are natural stress busters. These drinks can relieve anxiety and depression. On top of that, these fruit infused water recipes are delicious, relaxing, refreshing, and they have other health and weight loss benefits.

Relaxing Lemon and Cilantro

This drink is refreshing, and it helps relieve stress and anxiety. If you are going through a stressful phase in your life, this drink is for you.

Ingredients:

- 1 thinly sliced lemon

- 2 liters of drinking water

- Ice, if preferred

- ¼ cup of crushed cilantro

Combine the lemon, drinking water, cilantro, water, and ice in a large water pitcher. Gently stir using a spoon. Chill this stress-relieving drink in the refrigerator for about an hour before consuming.

Basil, Orange, and Lemon Water

This drink is delicious and it has a number of health benefits. This drink can relieve stress and anxiety. It is best to consume this fruit infused water after a long, tiring workday or whenever you feel stressed or agitated. This drink is rich in Vitamin C, too, so it can boost your metabolism.

Ingredients:

- 1 sliced lemon

- 1 sliced orange

- Ice, if preferred

- 20 ripped basil leaves

- 2 liters of drinking water

Combine the lemon, orange, basil leaves, ice, and drinking water in a large pitcher. You can consume this drink right away. But, for best results, chill this drink for about one hour in the refrigerator before consuming.

Stress-busting Raspberry, Blueberry, and Strawberry Infused Water

This is a very healthy, detoxifying drink that can also relieve stress and anxiety. This fruit infused water can also help improve your memory.

Ingredients:

- ½ cup of raspberries

- ½ cup of blueberries

- 2 liters of drinking water

- ½ cup of halved strawberries

- Ice, if preferred

Combine the blueberries, raspberries, water, strawberries, and ice in a large water pitcher. Stir using a wooden spoon or spatula. Chill in the refrigerator for about three hours before consuming.

Pear and Rosemary Stress-relieving Water

This is a very relaxing drink that can help relieve stress. This drink is just amazing and it has many other health benefits.

Ingredients:

- 2 sliced pears

- 2 liters of drinking water

- Ice, if preferred

- 2 sprigs of rosemary

Combine the pears, rosemary, drinking water, and ice in a large pitcher. Gently stir using a spoon. Chill in the refrigerator for about one hour before consuming.

Lemon, Cucumber, Lime, and Lemongrass Water

This drink has amazing stress-busting power. This drink is also rich in Vitamin C. This drink also has the ability to lower down your cholesterol level.

Ingredients:

- 2 stalks of lemongrass ·

- 1 thinly sliced cucumber

- 2 liters of drinking water

- Ice, if preferred

- 1 thinly sliced lime

- 1 thinly sliced lemon

Combine the cucumber, lemongrass, water, ice, lime, and lemon in a large water pitcher. Gently stir using a spoon or spatula. Chill in the refrigerator for about one hour before serving.

Kiwi, Strawberry, and Lemon Stress-Busting Water

This refreshing and relaxing drink relieves stress and helps you relax. This drink is rich in Vitamin C and it also cleanses the body.

Ingredients:

- 1 thinly sliced lemon

- 4 peeled and sliced kiwis

- 2 cups of halved strawberries

- Ice, if preferred

- 2 liters of drinking water

Combine the strawberries, lemon, and kiwis in a large water pitcher. Stir gently using a spoon or spatula. Chill this drink in a refrigerator before serving,

Relaxing Lavender and Lemon Water

This amazing infusion helps fight stress and anxiety. It also relieves the symptoms of Premenstrual Syndrome or PMS.

Ingredients:

- ¼ cup of lavender

- 2 liters of drinking water

- Ice, if preferred

- 3 thinly sliced lemon

Combine all the ingredients in a large water pitcher. Stir using a spoon or a spatula. Chill in the refrigerator for at least two hours before serving.

Rosemary and Blackberry Infused Water

This is a great stress-busting and relaxing drink. This fruit infused water is also rich in antioxidants and it has minerals that are good for the bones.

Ingredients:

- 1 cup of lightly crushed blackberries

- 1 liter of drinking water

- Ice, if preferred

- 4 sprigs of rosemary

Combine the water, blackberries, ice, and rosemary in a large pitcher. Stir using a spoon or a spatula. Chill in the refrigerator for at least an hour before serving.

Cherry, Ginger, and Lime Infused Water

This drink is relaxing and it relieves stress and anxiety. It is also good for the skin and it strengthens the immune system.

Ingredients:

- 2 inches of thinly sliced ginger root

- 1 thinly sliced lime

- Ice, if preferred

- 2 liters of drinking water

- 2 cups of sliced cherries

Place the lime, ginger, and cherries in a large water pitcher. Gently mix and muddle using a spatula or spoon to release the flavors. Add the water and Ice. Stir and chill in the refrigerator for at least an hour before serving.

Basil and Water Melon Fruit Infused Water

This is a relaxing fruit infused drink that is relaxing. This drink relieves stress and anxiety. You can consume this after a long day at work.

Ingredients:

- 10 basil leaves

- 1 liter of drinking water

- 2 cups of cubed seedless watermelon

- Ice, if preferred

Combine the water, ice, basil leaves, and cubed watermelon in a large pitcher. Chill in the refrigerator for about two hours before serving.

Rosemary Citrus Infused Water

Drinking this stress relieving drink is a great way to cap your day! This drink is also rich in Vitamin C and it can help you increase your metabolism and lose weight.

Ingredients:

- 1 thinly sliced lemon
- 3 crushed sprigs of rosemary
- 1 thinly sliced tangerine
- 1 thinly sliced lime
- 1 thinly sliced orange
- 1 thinly sliced lemon
- 2 liters of drinking water
- Ice

Place the rosemary, tangerine, lime, orange, and lemon in a large water pitcher. Muddle using a spoon to release the nutrients and flavors. Add water and stir. Refrigerate for about one hour before consuming. Place in beautiful glass bottles and serve with ice.

Basil and Mixed Berries Infused Water

This drink is therapeutic and it is rich in antioxidants. The basil relieves stress while the berries fight free radicals and help strengthen the immune system.

Ingredients:

- 10 basil leaves

- ½ cup of sliced strawberries

- ½ cup of sliced blueberries

- ½ cup of sliced blackberries

- 2 liters of drinking water

- Ice

Combine the basil leaves, strawberries, blueberries, and blackberries in a large water pitcher. Muddle gently using a spoon. Add the drinking water and refrigerate for about one hour before serving.

Basil, Banana, and Lemon Water

This drink is loaded with vitamins and minerals and it also helps you relax and battle stress and fatigue.

Ingredients:

- 1 sliced banana

- 10 torn basil leaves

- 1 liter of drinking water

- 1 lemon

Combine the banana, basil leaves, and lemon in a large water pitcher. Muddle lightly to release the flavors. Add the drinking water. Add ice, if preferred. Chill in the refrigerator for at least one hour before serving.

Plum, Blueberry, Apple, and Rosemary Water

This is a delicious detoxifying drink that can also relieve stress and anxiety. You can consume this in the morning or you can carry this around in a water bottle and consume this at work.

Ingredients:

- 1 cup of sliced plums

- 1 cup of sliced blueberries

- 2 crushed sprigs of rosemary

- 1 sliced apple

- 2 liters of drinking water

- Ice, if preferred

Combine the plums, blueberries, rosemary sprigs, and apple in a large water pitcher. Muddle lightly to release the nutrients and flavors. Add the water and ice. Chill in the refrigerator for about two hours before serving.

Cherry, Lime, and Basil Water

This is a refreshing drink that helps you relax after a long day at work.

Ingredients:

- 1 cup of halved cherries

- 2 thinly sliced limes

- 10 basil leaves

- 2 liters of drinking water

- Ice, if preferred

Combine the cherries, limes, water, basil leaves, and ice in a large pitcher. Stir gently using a spoon or a spatula. Chill in the refrigerator for about two hours before serving.

Rosemary, Cucumber, Strawberries, and Grapefruit Water

This is a relaxing fruit infused water that is loaded with vitamins and nutrients.

Ingredients:

- 1 thinly sliced cucumber

- 1 cup of sliced strawberries

- 1 sliced grapefruit

- 2 crushed sprigs of rosemary

- 2 liters of drinking water

- Ice, if preferred

Combine the cucumber, strawberries, rosemary, grapefruit, ice, and drinking water in a large pitcher. Stir using a spoon. Chill in the refrigerator for about two hours before serving.

Basil, Ginger, Orange, and Lemon Water

This is a flavorful citrus drink that can ease stress and boost metabolism. This is also refreshing and it is perfect for a long, hot, day.

Ingredients:

- 2 liters of drinking water

- 1 thinly sliced orange

- 1 thinly sliced lemon

- 1 inch ginger, peeled and sliced

- 10 basil leaves

- Ice, if preferred

Combine the orange, lemon, thinly sliced ginger, and basil leaves in a water pitcher. Muddle lightly using a spatula or spoon. Add the water and ice. Chill in the refrigerator for two hours before serving.

Carrots, Pomegranate, Cucumber, and Basil Water

This drink can calm you down and relieve stress.

Ingredients:

- 1 sliced pomegranate

- 1 sliced carrot

- 2 liters of drinking water

- 10 basil leaves

- 1 sliced cucumber

- Ice, if preferred

Combine the pomegranate, carrot, basil leaves, water, ice, and cucumber in a large water pitcher. Gently stir using a spoon. Chill in the refrigerator for about two hours before serving.

Cilantro, Lemon, Tangerine, and Hot Green Pepper Water

This drink helps relax the muscles and relieve the symptoms of stress and anxiety.

Ingredients:

- ½ cup of crushed cilantro leaves

- 2 liters of drinking water

- 1 thinly sliced lemon

- 1 thinly sliced tangerine

- 1 sliced green pepper

- Ice, preferred

Combine the cilantro leaves, lemon, tangerine, and green pepper in a large water pitcher. Muddle gently using a spoon. Add the water and ice. Chill in the refrigerator for at least one hour before serving.

Conclusion

Thank you again for downloading this book!

I hope this book was able to provide helpful information about the delicious and healthy fruit infused water. I hope that the recipes contained in this book are able to help you enjoy drinking more water. I also hope these recipes are able to help you lose weight, relieve stress, maintain a healthy and glowing skin, and remove harmful toxins from your body.

The next step is to make these delicious fruit infused drinks in the comfort of your home and enjoy these drinks anytime, anywhere.

Finally, if you enjoyed this book, please take the time to share your thoughts and post a positive review on Amazon. It'd be greatly appreciated!

With sincere thanks,

Lance Devoir

42179275R00068

Made in the USA
Lexington, KY
11 June 2015